Complicity
Eye Of The Storm

Leonard Charles Lee Collins

authorHOUSE®

AuthorHouse™ LLC
1663 Liberty Drive
Bloomington, IN 47403
www.authorhouse.com
Phone: 1-800-839-8640

Published by AuthorHouse   10/29/2013

ISBN: 978-1-4817-5577-1 (sc)
ISBN: 978-1-4817-5575-7 (e)

Library of Congress Control Number: 2013909723

Any people depicted in stock imagery provided by Thinkstock are models, and such images are being used for illustrative purposes only.
Certain stock imagery © Thinkstock.

This book is printed on acid-free paper.

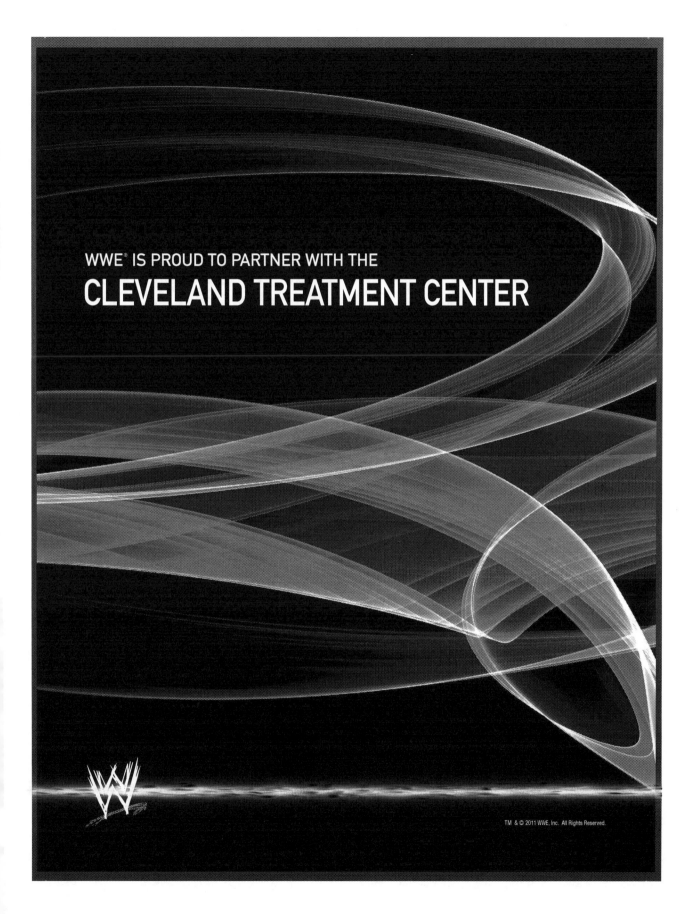

WWE® IS PROUD TO PARTNER WITH THE
CLEVELAND TREATMENT CENTER

MANAGING EDITOR:
PETER HOLMES , PRESIDENT/FOUNDER, DIRECTOR BUSINESS AFFAIRS

COPY EDITOR:
SUSAN TEMPLAR, DIRECTOR OF HUMAN RESOURCES/PREVENTION COORDINATOR

PUBLISHING MANAGEMENT:
CLEVELAND TREATMENT CENTER

PRODUCTION MANAGER:
LEONARD CHARLES LEE COLLINS, EXECUTIVE DIRECTOR

ART DIRECTORS:
RODNEY "ROCK" CARPENTER,
RESIDENT ARTIST
ARTISTS:
MARK MCQUEEN JR., ADMINISTRATIVE
SUPPORT MULTIMEDIA DESIGN
LEN L.C. COLLINS
MEDICAL/ILLUSTRATOR

WRITER:
SCRIBE L.C.

ALUMNI DIRECTOR:
DERRICK TURNER, SOCIAL NETWORK MANAGER

MULTIMEDIA COORDINATORS:
MARION LAWRENCE, CORPORATE COMPLIANCE OFFICER
MARK MCQUEEN JR.

ADVERTISING/SALES:
MIKE DREXLER
AD STORE USA, INC
239.482.5050

CIRCULATION/SUBSCRIPTION:
CLEVELAND TREATMENT CENTER
CTC1127@ATTGLOBAL.NET
WWW.THEJUSTCHILLINNATION.COM

SOCIETY FOR PREVENTION OF VIOLENCE
DAVID E. VOLOSIN, EXECUTIVE DIRECTOR
4645 RICHMOND RD., SUITE 103, WARRENSVILLE HTS., OHIO 44128
WWW.SPVOHIO.ORG

LETTERS TO THE EDITOR
COMPLICITYEOTS@GMAIL.COM

Complicity
Eye Of The Storm

Complicity
Eye Of The Storm

COME WITH ME COLLEAGUES AND FRIENDS OF THE JUST CHILLIN' NATION ON A JOURNEY THAT IS BOTH EDUCATIONAL AND ENTERTAINING. AS A FATHER, HUSBAND, AND BUSINESS MAN I FIND THAT MY PURPOSE IN LIFE HAS ALWAYS BEEN THE HEALTH AND SAFETY OF OTHERS. THIS HAS LEAD TO MY INVOLVEMENT WITH NUMEROUS COMMUNITY EFFORTS DIRECTED TOWARD EDUCATION, SUBSTANCE ABUSE, AND VIOLENCE PREVENTION JUST CHILLIN' ALLOWS ME THE OPPORTUNITY TO COLLABORATE WITH OTHERS THAT SHARE THE SAME MISSION, JUST CHILLIN' PROVIDES RESOURCES OF DIVERSE ORGANIZATIONS.

JUST CHILLIN' SOLVES THE PROBLEMS SOME YOUTH FACE WHEN CONFRONTED WITH LIFE CHOICES: WHAT BEHAVIORS ARE APPROPRIATE - BOTH IS SCHOOL AND BEYOND THE CLASSROOM. MANY YOUTH ARE ANGRY AND ACTING OUT THEIR FRUSTRATIONS. DRUGS, ALCOHOL AND SEX HAVE BECOME WEAPONS. ADOLESCENTS AND YOUNG ADULTS WITH LIMITED COPING AND DECISION-MAKING SKILLS TO MASK FAILURE; STRESS AND HOPELESSNESS TYPICALLY USE THEM. THESE STORIES GIVE THEM BOTH SOCIAL SKILLS AND SOCIAL TOOLS NEEDED TO ALIGN THEIR BEHAVIORS IN RESPONSE TO RAPID CHANGES IN THEIR SPACE.

BY LEVERAGING INFORMATION TECHNOLOGY AND INSERTING ITS USE INTO THE CULTURE CREATED AT THE INTERSECTION OF EDUCATION, MENTAL HEALTH, DRUG AND ALCOHOL ADDICTION, AWARENESS AND KNOWLEDGE WILL BE INCREASED. IMPORTANTLY, SOCIAL SKILLS DELIVERED VIA SOCIAL MEDIA CAN BE ADAPTED EASILY AND ADULTS CAN READILY MEASURE WHICH STORIES WORK AND THOSE THAT DO NOT. I MYSELF AS A WRITER TAKE GREAT JOY IN BEING ABLE TO SHARE STORIES THAT PROVIDE POSITIVE PATHS.

JUST CHILLIN' VALUES ARE REFLECTED IN OUR DAY-TO-DAY ACTIVITIES AS AN ORGANIZATION DESIGNED TO BE ABOUT THE BUSINESS OF PROVIDING QUALITY SERVICES. THE VALUES WE CHERISH MOST INCLUDE THE FOLLOWING: INTEGRITY, RESPECT, DIVERSITY OF APPRECIATION, EXCELLENCE, ADVOCACY, MARKET SENSITIVE, PROFESSIONAL, AND COLLABORATION.

SO SADDLE UP IF YOU ACCEPT OUR MISSION TO INSPIRE, CHALLENGE, AND EMPOWER OTHERS (I.C.E.) AND JOIN US AS WE STRIVE TO ENSURE THAT ALL YOUTH SHARE QUALITY, LIFE, AND HEALTH EXPERIENCES.

SINCERELY,

PETER HOLMES
MASTER SCRIBE

PROLOGUE

Matthew 5:5

In a hostile world, and where christians thrive
Storm clouds may gather

PLEASE ACCEPT ME, NOT AS THE EXECUTIVE DIRECTOR OF THE CLEVELAND TREATMENT CENTER, BUT AS SCRIBE L.C.; YOUR URBAN NAVIGATOR.

A YOUNG MAN I KNEW WAS DEAD BECAUSE OF HIS INVOLVEMENT WITH DRUG TRAFFICKING. I ATTENDED HIS FUNERAL, OR "GOING HOME" SERVICE. AS THE FUNERAL DIRECTOR SAID HE WAS GOING TO A "BETTER PLACE."

WEBSTER'S DICTIONARY DEFINES A FUNERAL AS A CEREMONY HELD FOR A DEAD PERSON, USUALLY BEFORE BURIAL. THE GOING HOME SERVICE IS MANAGED BY THE FUNERAL DIRECTOR WHO PREPARES THE DECEASED AT A FUNERAL HOME. THIS IS A SET OF ROOMS WITH FACILITIES FOR THE PREPARATION OF THE DEAD FOR BURIAL, CREMATION, OR FOR VIEWING THE BODY. FUNERAL HOMES ARE SOMETIMES A CHURCH, CREMATORY, OR OTHER TYPE OF GENERAL PURPOSE BUILDING PRESIDED OVER BY MEN AND WOMEN OF "FAITH" WHO COME TOGETHER IN PRAYER. A MINISTER, SOMETIMES A SPIRITUAL LEADER, GIVES AID OR SERVICE VIA *DIVINE GUIDANCE* CONCERNING ISSUES THAT GOVERN THE WAY WE LIVE. THIS IS DONE IN PREPARATION FOR DEATH AND TO ONE DAY LIVE AGAIN, SO WE CAN EITHER "GO HOME" OR GO TO A "BETTER PLACE".

A HOME IS THE HOUSE WHERE ONE LIVES, EITHER A DWELLING OR SOCIAL UNIT FORMED BY A FAMILY LIVING TOGETHER. A BETTER PLACE IS WHERE THE "LIVING" DWELL ALONG WITH THOSE WHO HAVE THEMSELVES FOR A LIFE AFTER DEATH, HEAVEN, OR A PLACE OR CONDITION CONTINUOUS HAPPINESS. SO THERE I WAS AT MY FRIEND'S FUNERAL. HE WAS DEAD, BUT ALIVE AND WAS GOING TO A BETTER PLACE.

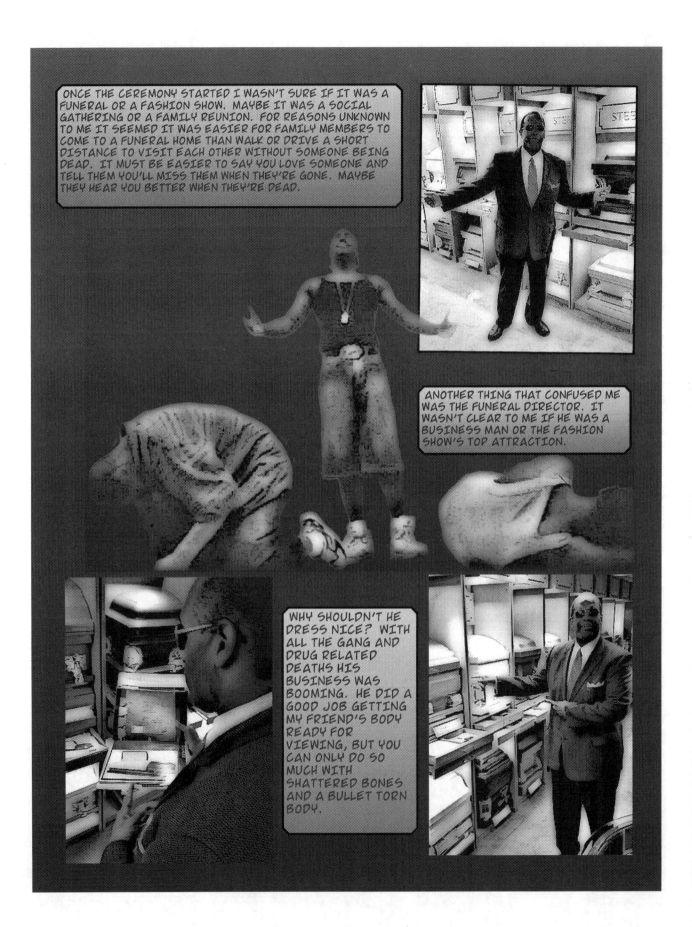

ONCE THE CEREMONY STARTED I WASN'T SURE IF IT WAS A FUNERAL OR A FASHION SHOW. MAYBE IT WAS A SOCIAL GATHERING OR A FAMILY REUNION. FOR REASONS UNKNOWN TO ME IT SEEMED IT WAS EASIER FOR FAMILY MEMBERS TO COME TO A FUNERAL HOME THAN WALK OR DRIVE A SHORT DISTANCE TO VISIT EACH OTHER WITHOUT SOMEONE BEING DEAD. IT MUST BE EASIER TO SAY YOU LOVE SOMEONE AND TELL THEM YOU'LL MISS THEM WHEN THEY'RE GONE. MAYBE THEY HEAR YOU BETTER WHEN THEY'RE DEAD.

ANOTHER THING THAT CONFUSED ME WAS THE FUNERAL DIRECTOR. IT WASN'T CLEAR TO ME IF HE WAS A BUSINESS MAN OR THE FASHION SHOW'S TOP ATTRACTION.

WHY SHOULDN'T HE DRESS NICE? WITH ALL THE GANG AND DRUG RELATED DEATHS HIS BUSINESS WAS BOOMING. HE DID A GOOD JOB GETTING MY FRIEND'S BODY READY FOR VIEWING, BUT YOU CAN ONLY DO SO MUCH WITH SHATTERED BONES AND A BULLET TORN BODY.

HE SIMPLY CLOSED THE CASKET. I DON'T THINK MOST OF THE PEOPLE AT THE FASHION NOTICED. MANY OF THE FAMILY MEMBERS HADN'T SEEM MY FRIEND IN 15 OF HIS LAST 19 YEARS. THE SERVICE STARTED AND THE MINISTER SEEMED TO CHARM THE CROWD. HE INSPIRED THEM WITH HIS CONSOLING SERMON. THE MESSAGE FOR THE LIVING WAS EVERYTHING WAS "COOL." THE DECEASED WAS GOING TO A "BETTER PLACE" BECAUSE THE RIGHT TIME IS THE RIGHT TIME. FOR A MINUTE OR SO THE **SERMON** WAS SOUNDING GOOD TO ME. I THOUGHT I COULD GET THIS "RIGHT TIME IS THE RIGHT TIME" THING. ALL I GOT TO DO IS GET KILLED. THEN I REMEMBERED I HAD SOMETHING SCHEDULED FOR LATER THAT EVENING. I ALSO STARTED WONDERING ABOUT MY FRIEND. DID HE HAVE ANY PLANSM ANY UNFINISHED BUSINESS? I KNOW HE WAS KILLED, BUT THAT IS SUPPOSED TO BE OK BECAUSE IT'S "THE RIGHT TIME".

I KNOW ITS DIFFICULT TALKING ABOUT VIOLENCE ESPECIALLY WHEN DEATH IS INVOLVED. BUT DAMN, ISN'T THIS SERMON SUPPOSED TO CONSOLE ME? TO MAKE IT EASIER FOR ME TO ACCEPT THE LOSS OF A FRIEND? I DON'T THINK SO BECAUSE I JUST CAN'T ACCEPT THAT "THE RIGHT TIME IS THE RIGHT TIME."

TO SEE YOUNG PEOPLE GETTIN' SMOKED (KILLED) FOR LESS THAN A DIME (THAT'S $10.00). YOUNG PEOPLE ON THE STREETS EXCHANGING THEIR BODIES FOR A NICKEL ($5.00) OR A CRUMB. A CRUMB IS NOT ENOUGH OF ANYTHING TO SATISFY ANY NEED. I CAN UNDERSTAND NOT HAVING MUCH, BUT WHAT IS NOT HAVING A CRUMB?

HITCHCOCK CENTER FOR Women INC

A Place Where Healing Begins

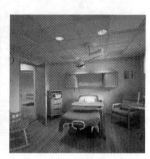

In the late 1970s, Jane Mazzarella, a nurse working at Cleveland's Women's General Hospital, began to recognize the prevalence of substance abuse among her patients. A strong advocate with ties to the recovery community, Ms. Mazzarella mustered the financial, political and grassroots support necessary to open a ten bed women's halfway house in 1978 . Hitchcock was originally housed in a home on Magnolia Drive donated by the Hitchcock family. The need for expanded space and treatment options exploded throughout the 1980s with the advent of crack cocaine. Through the continuing efforts of Ms. Mazzarella and the agency's board, staff and volunteers, the agency purchased the former St. Mary's Seminary on Ansel Road in Cleveland's near east side from the Cleveland Catholic Diocese in 1992.

At Hitchcock we have helped women for over 35 years on their journey of recovery from addiction. We do it the Hitchcock Way, offering a continuum of care - from intensive outpatient treatment to residential to a variety of housing services – for women and their children.

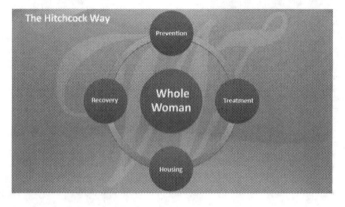

Our mission At Hitchcock is to wholistically empower women to achieve and maintain productive, chemically free lives at home, work, and in the community.

Hitchcock Center For Women
1227 Ansel Road
Cleveland, Ohio 44106
216.421.0662
info@hcfw.org
hcfw.org

Chapter 1:

THIS STORY BEGINS LIKE SO MANY OTHERS WITH SOMEONE'S CHILD STANDING AT THE **CROSSROADS**. QUENTIN A B+ STUDENT BROKE AS HELL, ON FINANCIAL AIDE, SHARING A CAR WITH HIS MOM AND MISSING THE FREE LUNCH HE GOT IN MARTIN LUTHER JR. KING HIGH SCHOOL.

LIKE **SCRIBES, HOMER, WALTER MOSLEY, DWAYNE MCDUFFLE** AND **MATTHEW**, I WILL ATTEMPT TO ADDRESS ISSUES OF "WRONG TIMES" THROUGH VISIONS OF PEOPLE AS THEY FACE THEM. THROUGH SERMONS, SONGS AND POEMS, THIS IS THEIR STORY. HOPEFULLY THIS TALE IS RELEVANT IN ANY PLACE, TIME OR LANGUAGE. IT'S ABOUT RELATIONSHIPS WITHIN THE EYE OF THE STORM OR IN THE HOOD. A SIMPLE QUESTION IS POSED BY WINDS OF CHANGE. A QUESTION THAT MUST BE ANSWERED. I HOPE THAT UNLIKE **CAIN** IN RESPONSE TO THE WIND'S QUESTION OF "WHERE IS THY BROTHER?" WE MUST HAVE A BETTER ANSWER ABOUT OUR CHILDREN THAN, "I KNOW NOT, AM I MY BROTHER'S KEEPER?" AS **MOSES** RECORDED IN **GENESIS** 7:9.

IT'S DIFFICULT TO ACCEPT THE TRUTH, I SUPPOSE THAT'S WHY WE SAY STOP THE VIOLENCE, STOP SELLING DRUGS AND TO STOP HAVING SEX. STOP EATING CANDY, STOP DRINKING MILK, AND THEN WE ASK "WHAT'S WRONG, DON'T YOU HAVE ANYTHING TO DO?" I "FORGOT, WE DO LET THEM GO TO SCHOOL BECAUSE "A MIND IS A TERRIBLE THING TO WASTE".

WHAT ABOUT TEACHING THEM THAT A LIFE IS A TERRIBLE THING TO WASTE AND A LIFE LOST TO VIOLENCE IS WRONG. ITS NEVER THE RIGHT TIME. LIFE IS THE GREATEST GIFT OF ALL. NO MATTER THE TRIALS AND TRIBULATIONS OR YOUR QUALITY OF LIFE. ITS SOMETHING VERY FEW DYING PEOPLE WOULD GIVE UP. LIFE IS A BLESSING WORTH LIVING AND THE STRUGGLES ALONG THE WAY CAN GIVE WAY TO HOPE AND TO A BETTER DAY. HOPE OF GOING TO A "BETTER PLACE," HOME. THAT'S WHERE PEOPLE LIVE. I THOUGHT, DAMN, IS LIFE THIS BAD? IS IT BECAUSE AS ADULTS, WHO HAVE "LIVED A LITTLE," WE FORGOT THAT LIFE IS WORTH LIVING, WORTH CONTINUING? WHY IS IT LITTLE CHILDREN LIVE, NOT WANTING TO GET OLD, TRYING NOT TO BECOME ADULTS? WHY IS IT THAT WE SO EASILY ACCEPT THE "RIGHT TIME IS THE RIGHT TIME?" WHY DO WE ACCEPT THAT THEY'RE "GOING TO A BETTER PLACE?"

IS THE RIGHT TIME BEING THE VICTIM OF A DRIVE BY SHOOTING? IS IT HAVING YOUR LIFE TAKEN BY DRUGS, AIDS OR BY DRINKING AND DRIVING? I DON'T THINK SO!

Psalm 84:10
Blessed is the man, who finds wisdom,
The man who gains understanding.

ALL THE RIGHTEOUSNESS IN THE WORLD ISN'T ALL THAT RIGHTEOUS IF WE CONTINUE TO ACCEPT THE LIVES OF OUR YOUNG PEOPLE BEING LOST TO VIOLENCE. I GUESS THE RIGHT TIME IS SOMETIMES THE WRONG TIME. "REST IN PEACE LITTLE BROTHA." PUMP YOUR FIST AND HOLLA' IF YOU HEAR ME.

Merriam Webster's Dictionary tells us that a Strom is a noun, often attributive to disturbance of the atmosphere marked by wind and usually by rain, snow, hail, sleet, or thunder and lightening. For Q is to be disturbed or agitated state (storm of emotions). Often followed by sudden violent commotion or tumultuous outburst (a storm of protests). Edge Water is his escape from the drama.

B.B. King sang "They called it Stormy Mondays, but Tuesday is just as bad. Oh, they called it stormy Monday, but Tuesday, Tuesday is just as bad. Oh Wednesday is worst and Thursday oh so sad." His words are so true because "all around the world," it's the "same song" as **Digital Underground** rapped. **Brook Benton** noted that when it's a rainy night in Georgia, "it seems like its raining all over the world." Far too many of us try to escape the rains of trouble by seeking refuge in the EYE OF THE STORM.

4

10

Black

Ministers, pastors, deacons, and trustees, sitting
in the store front church, from Philly to
N.Y.C., everyone is surviving their
personal storms, shouting and dancing
in the Spirit of the Lord, the ministry is flamboyant,
with the **Afrocentric** vision of **religious revival**,
from preachers who turn into congressmen, we
welcome our brothers from Sudan and everybody
smiles, the first female bishop is still waiting
for **generation X** to show up, it's not all
about **Iceberg Slim** and pushers, there is
more to me than what you see on T.V.,
my morals run deep, as I celebrate in my most
important community institution.

Dancing ministry
Flamboyant Afrocentric
African brothers

Alexander Ko

The typical family reunion within the Eye of the Storm, a funeral.

17

INDIVIDUALS OFTEN PUT UP A **PUBLIC FRONT** IN WHICH THEY CONVEY A FALSE **SELF-IMAGE** TO OTHERS. GENERALLY, ALL INDIVIDUALS WANT TO MAKE A GOOD IMPRESSION OF THEMSELVES. SO, THOSE INDIVIDUALS WANT TO CONFORM TO THE EXPECTATIONS OF OTHERS. THIS CAN HAPPEN IN ANY TYPE OF SOCIAL SETTING.

"**ERVING GOFFMAN'S DRAMATURGICAL ANALYSIS** DESCRIBES HOW INDIVIDUALS REACT "**THEATRICALLY**" IN SOCIAL INTERACTION.

INDIVIDUALS CREATE A **SELF-IMAGE**, SO THEY CAN GIVE A PREFERRED IMPRESSION OF THEMSELVES TO OTHERS.

JUST LET ME LOOK AT HIM. THAT'S MY CHILD. LORD, HAVE MERCY.

MY CHILD, THAT'S MY BABY. MY CHILD. I NEED TO SEE HIM ONE MORE TIME.

AS IN A THEATRICAL PERFORMANCE, THERE IS A FRONT WHERE A PUBLIC PERFORMANCE TAKES PLACE, AND A BACK STAGE WHERE THIS PERFORMANCE IS **CONTRADICTED**.

COME ON, MAMA. I KNOW THAT YOUR HEART IS BROKEN, BUT YOU'RE MAKING YOURSELF SICK.

THE BACK STAGE IS ALWAYS HIDDEN FROM THE FRONT STAGE PERFORMANCE AND FEW PEOPLE HAVE ACCESS TO IT."

20

LORD, WHEN IS THIS NONSENSE GOING TO STOP. WHEN ARE WE GOING TO LEARN HOW TO LIVE? LORD, YOU PROMISED US LIFE...

THE TRUTH OFTEN CREATES OBSTACLES IN THEIR SOCIAL RELATIONSHIPS WITH OTHERS.

GRIEVING PARENTS ARE GIVEN SUCH A SHORT TIME TO MAKE FUNERAL ARRANGEMENTS FOR CHILDREN LOST TO VIOLENCE.

YOU GOT THAT RIGHT PREACHER, AND ONE THING I KNOW ABOUT THE BIBLE IS THAT IT SAYS AN EYE FOR A MOTHERF#CKIN' EYE.

THE CONSIDERATIONS OF HER SON'S FRIENDSHIPS COMPROMISED HER **CONVICTIONS**. THE TRUTH IS AS GANG MEMBERS, THE **PALLBEARERS** WEREN'T ALLOWED IN HER HOME WHEN QUENTIN WAS ALIVE. MARION NOW FINDS HERSELF EMBARRASSED.

EMBARRASSED IT'S TOO LATE TO TRIP ABOUT HOODIES, CAPS, COLORS, HAND SIGNS AND LANGUAGE. HOW DISRESPECTFUL MARION THOUGHT. SHE WAS RAISED TO BELIEVE EVERYBODY HAD AN EASTER OUTFIT, WHITE SHIRTS AND TIES. THE TRUTH IS ITS NOT A REUNION. ITS A FUNERAL. SHE WISHED THEY WERE DRESSED IN ACCORDANCE.

THE LORD IS MY SHEPHERD. I SHALL NOT WANT. HE MAKETH ME TO LIE DOWN IN GREEN PASTURES. HE LEADETH ME BESIDE THE STILL WATERS. HE RESTORETH MY SOUL...

YEAH, THOUGH I WALK THROUGH THE VALLEY OF THE SHADOW OF DEATH, I WILL FEAR NO EVIL...

LETS NOT FORGET PASTOR SALEM SIMON CANCELED THE CHURCH'S RETREATS; YOUTH WERE GAMBLING ON *MADDEN VIDEO GAMES*. THE SUMMER FREE LUNCH PROGRAMS ENDED BECAUSE KIDS DIDN'T COME THE FIRST WEEK OF EACH MONTH.

22

23

Boo-Yah!

I'M GONE MOVE ON RIGHT AFTER SOME MOTHERF#CKIN' GET BACK. AND, I'M GONE LET MY MOTHERF#CKIN' GAT DO MY TALKING. IT SPEAKS 49 DIFFERENT LANGUAGES, TOO.

JASON PETRISH NOTES THAT ITS NOT ALWAYS "THE MAN'S" FAULT. SOMETIMES WE ARE IMPRISONED BY OUR OWN ACTIONS.

Prisoner In My Own Skin
I'm innocent, I've done no crime,
I've been here for such a long time.
Incarcerated with scarred hearts and faces,
My people defeated in the war of the races.
We were once kings and queens,
With many hopes and dreams.
Converted to criminals and crack fiends,
With no means of being redeemed.
I'm trapped in the hood, so it seems,
My only means of upward mobility is if I make it big on the radio or T.V.
They make it seem like they want me to be free,
But count how many times they've failed to help me.
I was promised 40 acres and a mule,
Just so I'd follow their rules.
Serious contemplation led me to believe segregation
Was designed and created to make my chances slim.
Don't see why I can't win,
It's simple, I'm a prisoner in my own skin.

27

DAMN OSCAR LIKE TUPAC IS "TIRED OF FEELING SAD TIRED OF PUTTING IN WORK AND TIRED OF CRYING WATCHING MY HOMIES LEAVE THE EARTH." *W.E.B. DUBOIS* STATED IN *"SOULS OF BLACK FOLKS"* THAT "THE ULTIMATE VALIDATION OF ONE'S WORTH IS KNOWING THAT YOU ARE NOT ALONE, THAT THERE IS SOMEONE ELSE JUST LIKE YOU."

IT'S ALL ABOUT YOUR BROTHER. IT'S ABOUT OUR COLORS, AND IT'S ABOUT GETTING RESPECT. WE DON'T NEED YOUR PERMISSION TO GO OUT AND KILL US A MOTHERF#CKER. YOU GOT TO HAVE HEART.

"SMOKIN BLUNT AFTER BLUNT AND STEADY DRINKIN" OSCAR SEES THAT DRAMA BLINDS THEM. THE NEED FOR REVENGE IS WHAT DRIVES THEM. THE PLAN IS TO "RETALIATE AND PULL A 187."

IT'S TIME FOR A NIGGA TO KILL. A NIGGA GOT TO GO DOWN FOR THIS, AND I GOT ENOUGH HEART TO TAKE HIM DOWN.

WHERE IS MY BROTHER'S HEART? WHERE IS MY MOTHER'S HEART? BROKEN. GO TELL HER ABOUT HEART WHEN ALL SHE KNOWS IS HEARTACHE. HOW LONG WILL IT BE BEFORE IT'S NOBODY LEFT? HOW MANY MOTHER'S HEARTS GOT TO BREAK BEFORE IT ALL STOPS? WHAT ABOUT YOUR MOTHER? YOU EVER THINK ABOUT HOW IT'S GOING TO BREAK HER HEART WHEN THEY GET BACK AROUND TO KILLING YOU?

THEY DON'T HEAR HIM TRYING TO MAKE AMENDS OSCAR KNOWS HE IS LOSING ALL HIS FRIENDS.

LIKE TUPAC, "ITS KINDA HARD TO BE OPTIMISTIC WHEN HIS BROTHER WAS LYING DEAD ON THE PAVEMENT TWISTED."

28

TEMIA WILKERSON AND JASON PETRISH, LET IT RIDE SCRIBES, ONCE WROTE LETTERS OF APPRECIATION TO ACKNOWLEDGE THE PERSON WHO NEVER GAVE UP ON THEM. THEIR WORDS ARE SIMILAR TO THOSE OSCAR NOW UNDERSTANDS. IF NOT FOR THE JUDGE AND HIS MOTHER HE TOO WOULD BE LOST.

LETTER OF APPRECIATION

"THE NUMBER ONE PERSON IN MY LIFE IS MY MOTHER. MY MOTHER ALWAYS FOUND A WAY TO INSPIRE ME ON EVERYTHING I DO. WHEN I WAS YOUNGER, I NEVER KNEW HOW MUCH MY MOTHER HAD A BIG EFFECT ON MY LIFE BY BEING THERE FOR ME MOST WHEN I NEEDED HER. RIGHT NOW I WOULD SAY SHE IS MY BEST FRIEND AND I APPRECIATE EVERYTHING SHE HAS DONE FOR ME.

MY MOTHER IS LIKE MY GUARDIAN ANGEL. SHE WATCHES OVER ME EVEN WHEN WE ARE NOT EVEN TOGETHER. SHE KNOWS EVERYTHING I'M GOING TO DO BEFORE I DO IT. THAT'S HOW MUCH MY MOTHER LOVES ME, AND I LOVE HER FOR THAT. MY MOTHER IS MY EVERYTHING. I COULD NEVER GIVE BACK TO MY MOTHER WHAT SHE GAVE ME, AND THAT WAS HER TIME, HER MONEY, HER HEART, AND HER GENTLE KISS. I LOVE MY MOTHER WITH ALL MY HEART, AND I GREATLY APPRECIATE EVERYTHING SHE HAS DONE FOR ME."

TEMIA WILKERSON

ALWAYS BESIDE ME

"YOU ARE CONSTANTLY ON MY CASE. YOU ARE ALWAYS RIDING ME ABOUT SOMETHING. IT SEEMS AS IF I CAN'T DO ANYTHING RIGHT BY YOU. IT'S ALWAYS: DO THIS, HE DID THAT, YOU FORGOT TO DO THIS, HE'LL FORGET TO DO THAT, AND SO ON AND SO ON. DAD, YOU BLAME ME FOR EVERYTHING AND RARELY GIVE ME FULL CREDIT FOR THINGS I DO WELL. IT REALLY GETS ME THINKING THAT YOU DON'T THINK ANYTHING THAT I DO IS GOOD ENOUGH. BUT NOW I AM GROWN, AND ALTHOUGH I KNEW IT BEFORE – I REALIZE NOW THE REASONS WHY YOU ARE THIS WAY. I KNOW YOU WANT THE BEST FOR ME AND FOR ME TO BE THE BEST I CAN BE. ALTHOUGH I DON'T FULLY UNDERSTAND WHY YOU ARE LIKE THIS WITH ME, I DO, HOWEVER, KNOW THAT DEEP DOWN YOUR INTENTIONS ARE GOOD AND FOR MY OWN BENEFIT. FOR THIS DAD, I WANT TO THANK YOU. BECAUSE OF YOUR (SOMETIMES TOUGH) LOVE, I AM PROUD OF THE MAN I HAVE BECOME, AND I AM PROUD TO BE YOUR SON."

JASON PETRISH

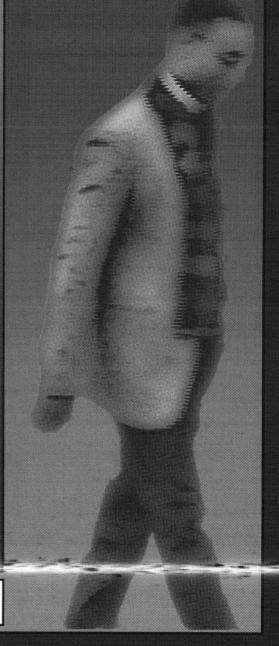

I AGREE WITH **PROVERBS 3:13**, "BLESSED IS THE MAN, WHO FINDS WISDOM, THE MAN WHO GAINS UNDERSTANDING." YES THAT IS OSCAR.

HOLD UP A MINUTE. WE GOT'S TO RECORD OUR HISTORY. Q NAME GOT TO GO UP ON THE WALL.

AIN'T Y'ALL GONE SHOW SOME LOVE FOR Q? BETTER RECOGNIZE.

RESEARCHERS IN 1985 FOUND THAT CHILDREN WHO SCORED HIGH ON FIRST GRADE READINESS AN IQ TESTS EXHIBITED EARLIER AND MORE FREQUENT USE OF ALCOHOL AND MARIJUANA.

SIMILAR TO THEIR FOREFATHERS, YOUNG AFRICAN-AMERICAN MALES FACE MAJOR CHALLENGES TO THEIR DEVELOPMENT AND WELL-BEING. CURRENT SOCIAL AND ECONOMIC INDICATORS OF BLACK MALE DEVELOPMENT PROVIDE A PROFILE OF AN INDIVIDUAL WHOSE QUALITY OF LIFE AND HEALTH IS IN SERIOUS JEOPARDY. IN RECENT YEARS, BLACK MALES HAVE BEEN REFERRED TO AS AN "ENDANGERED SPECIES", A "MENACE TO SOCIETY", AND "AMERICA'S MOST WANTED".

CHECK OUT. AIN'T THAT ONE OF THEM MOTHERF#CKERS THAT TOOK OUT Q?

I TAKE IT THAT YOU MUST BE LOST BECAUSE I KNOW THAT YOU AIN'T GOT THE NERVE TO BE DISRESPECTING US CROSSING US WITH THEM COLORS.

ENTER DEVIN COLLINS AN HONOR STUDENT AND ALL LEAGUE TRACK RUNNER. WITHOUT A SAFETY PLAN HE SEES A CROWD SHOOTING DICE ON HIS WAY HOME.

DEVIN DOESN'T GAMBLE PLUS THERE IS PLENTY OF SPACE TO MAKE HIS WAY THROUGH.

MAYBE A TEACHER PARENT OR A FRIEND WARNED HIM THAT WHEN YOU SEE A GROUP **FRONTING**, **COLORS**, **FLAGGING**, GAMBLING, AND DRINKING USE **COMMON SENSE** CROSS THE STREET OR TAKE AN ALTERNATIVE ROUTE.

31

32

33

A WEEK LATER, ANOTHER FAMILY REUNION; THIS TIME ITS THE FRANKLINS. DR. DEBORAH PROTHROW-STITH IN HER BOOK "DEADLY CONSEQUENCES" STATED THAT MINORITY MALES AGES 15 AND OLDER, DIE IN HOMICIDES SEVEN TIMES MORE FREQUENTLY THAN YOUNG WHITE MALES.72% OF THOSE VICTIMS CRIMINAL HOMICIDE WERE MURDERED BY *ACQUAINTANCES*." THEY WERE KILLED BY PEOPLE THEY KNEW., MAD CITY NOW RECOGNIZED AFTER KILLING DEVIN THAT HE AND HIS TEAMMATES ATTENDED QUENTIN'S FUNERAL. EVERYONE KNOWS MAD CITY PUTS IN WORK AT THE TRACK MEETS IF YOU NEED A LICK.

THEY KNEW MY BABY RAN TRACK AND WASN'T IN A DAMN GANG.

MY HUSBAND, IS A *SOCIAL WORKER*,IM AN ,WE BOTH GREW UP IN THIS COMMUNITY.

WE WERE MEMBERS OF THE CARDINALS MARCHING BAND. AS ALUMNI AND WITH DEVIN ON THETRACK TEAM, WE ATTENDED EVERY MEET, TO SUPPORT ALL THE KIDS.

WHEN IS IT GONNA STOP. LORD JESUS, FIRST MY QUENTIN, NOW YOUR SON.

DEVINS PARENTS MR AND MRS FRANKLIN, QUESTION THEIR DECISION TO RAISE THEIR CHILDREN HERE ON MLK, THE NEIGHBORHOOD THEY LOVE.

34

Others call it the hood or projects, for us its simply home.

MLK Boulevard: Urban Navigator

"Verily. The old heavens have vanished."

This urban firmament, Martin Luther King Jr. Boulevard is not what prophetic eyes envisioned.

Is equality another solar promise unanswered?

Can you feel my pain?

So many caught up in the insane.

Calm metamorphosis gives way to cosmic slop.

Gotham cities, emergency stations whose oppressive carousels never stop.

Like the sun eclipsed by the moon, I walk in the cold condemned by the Milky Way.

Yet, Martin Luther King Jr. Boulevard, your name gives testimony of the being a better day.

So many fear you at the midnight hour.

One wonders about the realities of power.

So I ride, walk, and even run across you, my concrete mile.

You flow through the "dark continents" like an Apocalypse, with me on your back, next to me sits my ebony child.

You make my travels a bit easier today.

I read your posted signs that direct me along my way.

I have seen your messages that many fail to see.

So I clue in my baby, its my responsibility.

In a time not too long ago, our paths were blocked by the snow.

So I sing "Verily, he old heavens have vanished," they had to go.

As your descendant, your name inspires me to remember my duty to teach and remind this child I'm rearing and riding. My stop is around the corner the crossroads lay beyond the clearing. So I thank you for helping me along the way.

You've been my "drinking gourd" this day.

Chapter 4: Can We Get A Witness

ELSEWHERE, POLICE HEADQUARTERS. *HOMICIDE* INTERVIEW ROOM

DETECTIVE SCOTT I GREW UP IN THE HOOD WE JUST KEEP HOLDING ON, LIKE THAT *BRAND NUBIAN* SONG. YOU KNOW THE WORDS.

"YEAH, SHOT HIM AND HE DROPPED, LIKE A BEANBAG MEAN *********** WITH A RAG AND SOME JEANS THAT SAG THEY SIGNIFY YOUR DEATH BY CROSSIN OUT YOUR TAG THEN THEY GO AND BRAG THAT THEY TOOK ANOTHER LIFE NEVER TO THINK, DO A BROTHER GOT A MOTHER AND A WIFE?"

RUN-INS WITH THE LAW ARE SO COMMON AMONG YOUNG MALES THAT THE STIGMA ASSOCIATED WITH BEING LOCKED UP IS GONE. IT'S HOW THEY ROLL. ITS COOL TO HAVE A PAROLE OFFICER.

"YOUNG BLACK MALE, TWENTY-FIVE YEARS OF AGE MANY-A-LIVES DIDN'T SURVIVE TO THIS STAGE CAUSE THE RAGE OF ANOTHER BROTHER GOT HIM POPPED" BRO YOU KNOW THE REST.

DAMN, IT TOOK THREE WEEKS TO MAKE ARRESTS. BECAUSE SOME OF THEIR FAMILIES FEEL ALIENATION FROM THE DOMINANT VALUES OF SOCIETY "IT'S THE WHITE MAN'S WORLD" THEY LIED AND HID THEM. GOOD PEOPLE LIKE MRS.ALLEN WHO WITNESS THE KILLING KEPT CALLING. GOD BLESS THEM.

HOMICIDE DETECTIVES SCOTT AND TEMPLAR CONTINUE THEIR INTERVIEWS WITH MAD CITY. ITS A SIMPLE GAME, GOOD COP VS BAD COP. THEIR GOAL IS TO IDENTIFY THE VARIOUS PLAYERS AND THEIR ROLES IN THE DEATH OF DEVIN FRANKLIN.

38

THIS IS GOING NOWHERE, GET HIM OUT OF HERE.

DETECTIVE SCOTT, THESE KIDS DON'T UNDERSTAND WHAT THE LEGAL SYSTEM IS. DAMN, THEY'RE LIKE THE THREE MUSKETEERS. ALL FOR ONE AND ONE FOR ALL. GUARD, BRING THE NEXT ONE IN TO INTERVIEW.

THEY ARE PLAYERS IN VARIOUS CRIMINAL ENTERPRISES. THIS POSITION COMPRISES JUSTICE AND LIKE MICHAEL FRANTI NOTES, "SILENCE IS THE LANGUAGE OF VIOLENCE". THE QUESTION IS ARE YOU A SNITCH OR A GOOD NEIGHBOR? TRAP, IS NOT A GOOD NEIGHBOR.

T-MAN IS THE NEXT TO BE INTERVIEWED. WHEN HE JOINED MAD CITY HE BECAME THE ENFORCER. EVERYONE SPENDS A LOT OF TIME TALKING ABOUT THE IMPORTANCE OF ROLE MODELS WHENEVER PRESENTING WAYS TO HELP YOUTH PRACTICE POSITIVE BEHAVIORS. T-MAN IS CONSIDERED AN ORIGINAL GANGSTER OR OG. HE'S A ROLE MODEL FOR SOME. "THE KIND OF "G" THE LITTLE HOMIES WANNA BE LIKE" RAPS COOLIO.

DETECTIVE TEMPLAR, LET ME REINTRODUCE T-MAN. YOU REMEMBER HIM, HE WAS HERE DURING THE GANG TRUCE WE CALLED AFTER QUENTIN HOLMES WAS KILLED. T-MAN KNOWS HOW WE GET DOWN, THOSE *PERPETRATORS* HAVE BEEN LOCKED UP.

GRAB A SEAT AND LEAVE THE GANG SIGNS AT THE DOOR.

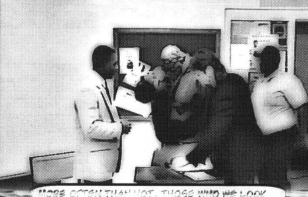

MORE OFTEN THAN NOT, THOSE WHO WE LOOK TO, TO FILL THESE ROLES ARE PEOPLE WHO HAVE REACHED SUPER STARDOM OR ARE SO UNREAL OR DEAD THAT THEY ARE INACCESSIBLE.

INFORMANTS, SNITCHES, RATS, ARE NOT *ROLE MODELS*, THEY ARE DISLOYAL VIOLATORS OF TRUST. DON'T HATE THE REAL PLAYERS, PEOPLE WHO REPORT CRIME TO THE AUTHORITIES, HATE THE GAME. THE GAMES NEVER CHANGES, ONLY THE PLAYERS. WHEN WE SPEAK OF THE "*GOOD OLD DAYS*" THERE WAS CRIME, *SNOOPS* LYRICS "GIN AND JUICE" ISN'T *ONE SCOTCH, ONE BOURBON, AND ONE BEER* THAT *JOHN LEE HOOKER* PREFER, BUT ITS ALCOHOL. THE *HYPOCRISY IS* THAT *MUDDY WATERS, RICK JAMES* AND *DR. DRE* SANG ABOUT THE LOVE OF THE CHRONIC.

40

41

YOUTH NEED POSITIVE EXAMPLES OF PERSONAL, SPIRITUAL, CULTURAL, EMOTIONAL, HISTORICAL, SOCIAL, POLITICAL, MENTAL, AND PHYSICAL *RITES OF PASSAGES* TO ASSIST IN MAKING THE TRANSITION TO "RESPONSIBLE" ADULTHOOD.

THE LIFE EXPERIENCES OF ONES ANCESTORS AND ELDERS IS A "REAL" MODEL OF THE SKILLS RELATED TO THE PERSONAL TASKS NECESSARY FOR EXERCISING ADULT RESPONSIBILITY AND SURVIVAL. STREET LAWYERS, REGULATORS, AND DRUG DEALERS ARE NOT *LEGAL COUNSELOR, CHIEF EXECUTIVE OFFICERS*, OR *PHARMACIST*.

REAL TALK A LOT OF KIDS ARE FREQUENTLY THE VICTIMS OF NEGATIVE ATTITUDE AND LOWERED EXPECTATIONS FROM THEIR FAMILY, COMMUNITY, PEERS, TEACHERS, COUNSELORS, AND EMPLOYERS YET THAT'S NEVER AN EXCUSE TO KILL. THOSE NEGATIVE PUBIC AND SOMETIMES SELF-IMPOSED ATTITUDES DOOM BOTH OUR YOUTH AND ADULT TO A SELF-FULFILLING *PROPHECY* OF UNDER-ACHIEVEMENT, FRUSTRATION, AND FAILURE.

IF ONLY THE YOUTH LISTEN TO WHAT POSITIVE ADULTS LIKE CURTIS MAYFIELD HAD TO SAY. "HOW LONG HAVE YOU HATED YOUR WHITE TEACHER, WHO TOLD YOU, YOU LOVE YOUR BLACK PREACHER, CAN YOU RESPECT YOUR BROTHER'S WOMAN FRIEND AND SHARE WITH BLACK FOLKS NOT OF KIN?

WE CANNOT CONTINUE TO ALLOW ILL-PREPARED YOUTH TO DESTROY ENTIRE FAMILIES BECAUSE OF NEGATIVE CHOICES SUCH AS, "BEING TRUE TO THE GAME".

THEY TRIED TO SWEAT ME, TOO. YOU JUST GOT TO PLAY THEIR GAME. "LOOK BOSS, IF I HAD SOMETHING TO TELL YOU, I WOULD. BUT I AIN'T GOT SHIT TO TELL."

I JUST HOPE THAT BOTH YOU NIGGAS HELD OUT FOR YOUR OWN SAKES.

WE TALKING ABOUT MURDER, MAN. WE TALKING ABOUT SOME PUNK ASS OPEN HIS MOUTH AND GO SOFT, WE'RE GOING DOWN FOR A 1-8-7.

ALL I NEED TO KNOW IS THAT YOU HELD IT DOWN.

WHAT? DO YOU THINK I'M A B*TCH? YOU KNOW T-MAN GOT HEART. THEY CAN'T PLAY ME OUT OF THE PACK LIKE THAT.

G-ROCK IS STILL STUCK ON STUPID HE REFUSES TO UNDERSTAND THAT THERE ARE WAYS BESIDES VIOLENCE TO MEDIATE A DIFFERENCE.

MAD CITY MADE A PLAN WHILE DRINKING AND GETTING HIGH. THEY MUST UNDERSTAND THAT IF YOU MAKE A MISTAKE YOU MUST LEARN FROM THAT MISTAKE AND TO KEEP ON KEEPING ON UNTIL IT'S CORRECTED OR MANAGEABLE.

DENIAL OF THE STREET CODE "DONT DO THE CRIME IF YOU CANT DO THE TIME," IS A BAD PLAN .THE CONSEQUENCES OF ONES ACTS MUST BE CONSIDERER.

Chapter 5: Stop, Look and Listen.

SIX MONTHS LATER WE FIND MAD CITY HAS JUST COMPLETED THAT LONG RIDE DOWN INTERSTATE 71.

THEY'VE REACHED THEIR HOME FOR THE NEXT 40 YEARS AT MANSFIELD CORRECTIONAL INSTITUTION.

SGT. DON DAVIS IS LOCKED AND LOADED TO PROCESS THE NEW ARRIVALS.

THE WALLS OF THE PRISON ARE A *SOBERING* SITE FOR ALL THE PASSENGERS RIDING IN THE STATE TRANSPORTATION VEHICLE.FOR MAD CITY THEIR LIVES OF LIES AND PERPETRATING FALSE IDENTITIES ARE COMING TO AN END.THEIR PARTY IS OVER.

"IT IS IMPOSSIBLE TO CALCULATE THE MORAL MISCHIEF, IF I MAY SO EXPRESS IT , THAT MENTAL LYING HAS PRODUCED IN SOCIETY. WHEN A MAN HAS SO FAR CORRUPTED AND PROSTITUTED THE CHASTITY OF HIS MIND AS TO SUBSCRIBE HIS PROFESSIONAL BELIEF TO THINGS HE DOES NOT BELIEVE,HE HAS PREPARED HIMSELF FOR THE COMMISSION OF EVERY OTHER CRIME."
~THOMAS PAINE

STANDING NAKED AND COLD IN THE MIDST OF A CAVITY SEARCH THE TRUTH IS BECOMING CLEARER.

"A LIE MAY TAKE CARE OF THE PRESENT, BUT IT HAS NO FUTURE". IT AIN'T NO GAME, ITS PLAIN TO SEE.

WE GOT TO GET PAST TELLING OUR YOUTH TO DO AS I SAY (RIGHT) AND NOT AS I DO (WRONG). AS SPITTED BY *M.C. BREED* "AIN'T NO FUTURE IN YO FRONTING."

G-ROCK'S FEELINGS ARE ELOQUENTLY EXPRESSED IN THE LYRICS OF *AKON, "THEY WON'T LET ME OUT, I'M LOCKED UP.* 'CAUSE VISITATION NO LONGER COMES BY, SEEMS LIKE THEY FORGOT ABOUT ME." HE CONSIDERS THE FACT THAT HE'S NOW AN HOUR AND A HALF AWAY FROM HOME. WHEN HE WAS JUST DOWNTOWN, IT WAS DIFFICULT FOR HIS FAMILY TO COME AND SEE HIM

MICHELLE ALEXANDER REMINDS US IN HER WORK *"THE NEW JIM CROW LAWS"* THAT THE NUMBER OF AFRICAN AMERICAN MALES INVOLVED IN THE CRIMINAL JUSTICE SYSTEM IS A DIRECT PARADOX TO THE ACHIEVEMENTS OF BLACKS IN AMERICA. MAD CITY JUST MURDERED A KID ON THE GROUNDS OF JOHN MCLENDON PARK WHO IS RECOGNIZED AS THE FIRST AFRICAN AMERICAN BASKETBALL COACH AT A PREDOMINANTLY WHITE UNIVERSITY. . MAD CITY AND "BROTHAS" OF COLOR, TOASTED IN CELEBRATION WHEN BARACK OBAMA WAS ELECTED PRESIDENT. OTHER POSITIVE IMAGES INCLUDE *DR. BEN CARSON, NEUROSURGEON; GENERAL COLIN POWELL; TYLER PERRY, PRODUCER AND WRITER; VIKTOR SCHRECKENGOST, DESIGNER; WALTER MOSLEY, WRITER AND DENNY COWEN, COMIC WRITER.*

STILL WITH ALL THESE IMAGES OF SUCCESS, OUR YOUTH ARE EXPOSED TO DAILY EXAMPLES THAT SUPPORT THE FACT THAT MORE AFRICAN AMERICAN MEN ARE IN PRISON OR JAIL, ON PROBATION OR PAROLE THAN WERE ENSLAVED IN 1850, BEFORE THE CIVIL WAR BEGAN. ~MICHELLE ALEXANDER.

ALTHOUGH ITS A JOB SGT. DON DAVIS HAS BEEN DOING FOR THE LAST 25 YEARS. HE IS SICKENED BY THE FACT THAT THE PERPETRATORS KEEP GETTING YOUNGER AND YOUNGER.

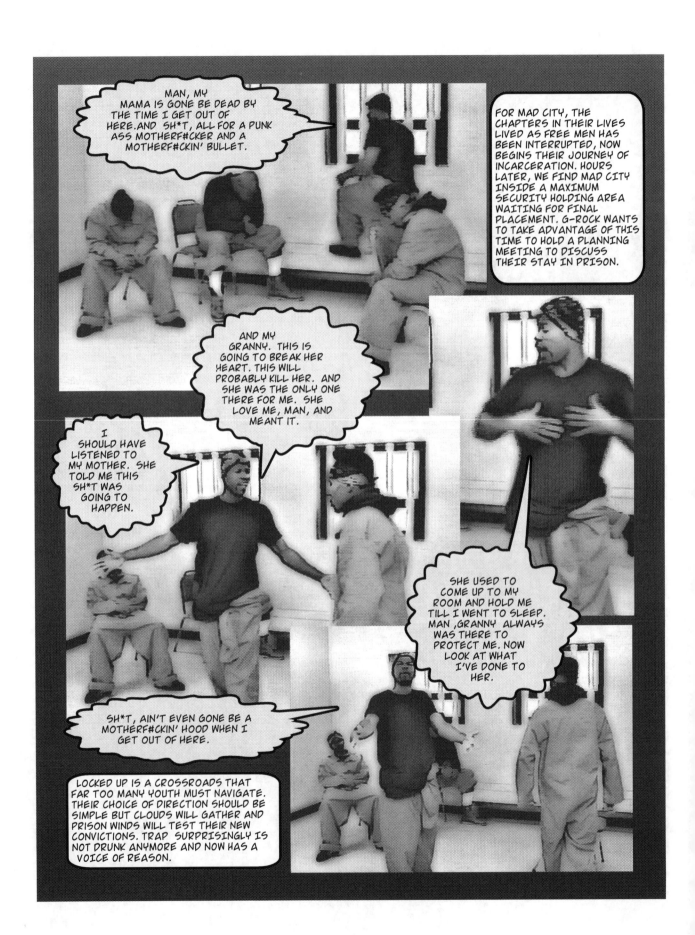

51

52

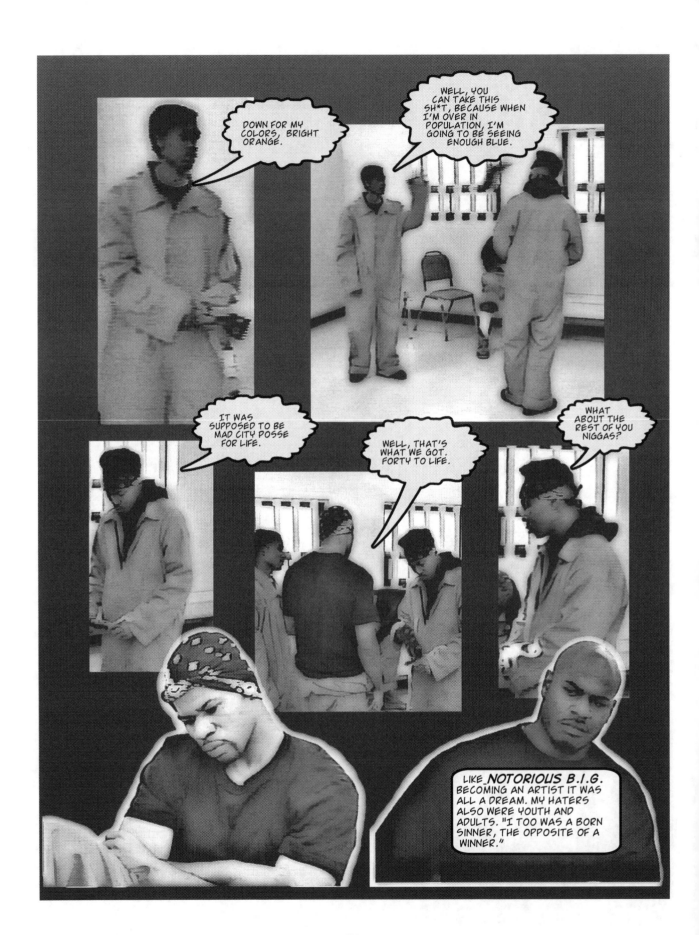

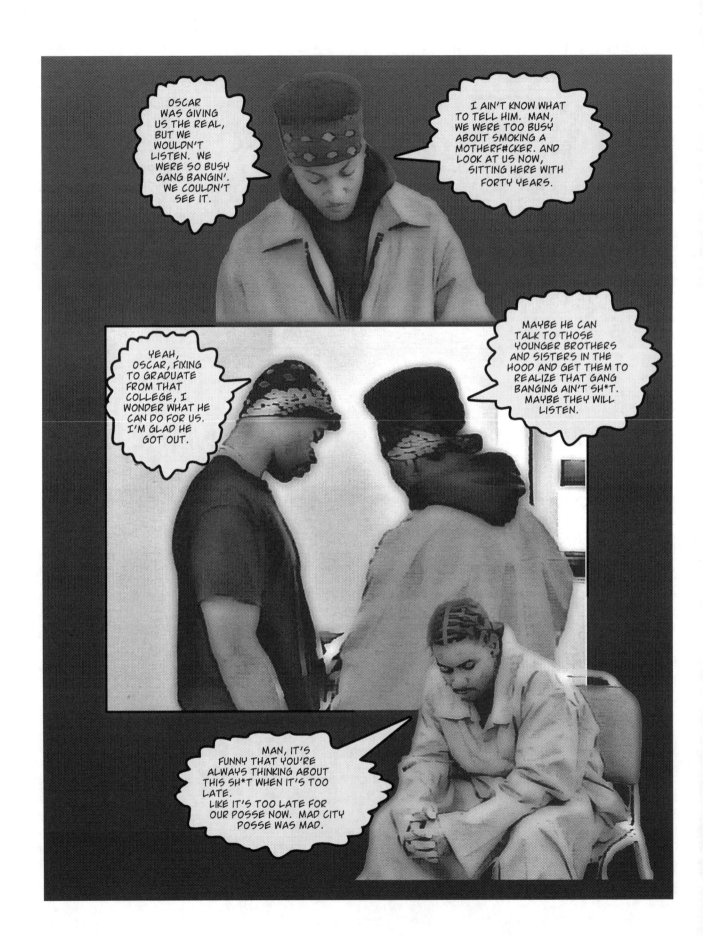

56

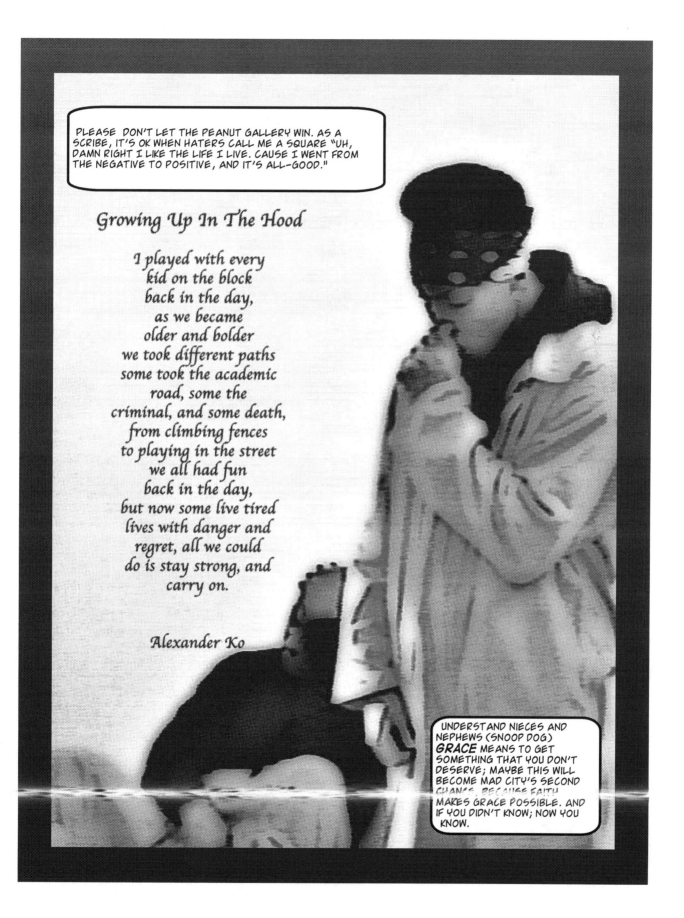

PLEASE DON'T LET THE PEANUT GALLERY WIN. AS A SCRIBE, IT'S OK WHEN HATERS CALL ME A SQUARE "UH, DAMN RIGHT I LIKE THE LIFE I LIVE. CAUSE I WENT FROM THE NEGATIVE TO POSITIVE, AND IT'S ALL-GOOD."

Growing Up In The Hood

I played with every
kid on the block
back in the day,
as we became
older and bolder
we took different paths
some took the academic
road, some the
criminal, and some death,
from climbing fences
to playing in the street
we all had fun
back in the day,
but now some live tired
lives with danger and
regret, all we could
do is stay strong, and
carry on.

Alexander Ko

UNDERSTAND NIECES AND NEPHEWS (SNOOP DOG) **GRACE** MEANS TO GET SOMETHING THAT YOU DON'T DESERVE; MAYBE THIS WILL BECOME MAD CITY'S SECOND CHANCE, BECAUSE FAITH MAKES GRACE POSSIBLE. AND IF YOU DIDN'T KNOW; NOW YOU KNOW.

Parenting with Love and Limits® – PLL

KEY COMPONENTS

The average service duration is 7 to 9 months, depending on the youth's length of stay in out-of-home care. Services begin at the time of commitment to the placement and continue for 90 days following discharge from the placement. A PLL team can serve up to 30 families annually and consists of a Master's Level Therapist and a Bachelor's level Case Manager. PLL provides bi-weekly supervision for the Therapist and Case Manager, and sessions are videotaped and reviewed by PLL clinical staff to ensure adherence to the model.

SERVICE FOR YOUTH IN OUT-OF-HOME CARE

- *Group/Individual Therapy for Parents:* Parents participate in 6 weekly 2 hour sessions in their local community and individual sessions as needed to prepare for youth returning home
- *Family Therapy:* 8 family therapy sessions are conducted either via videoconference or in person depending on the location of the youth's placement, including an emphasis on trauma-informed care
- *After-Care Plan:* At Family Therapy Session 4, an individualized Playbook is developed for the family to prepare for the youth's return home
- *Benchmark Meeting:* The Therapist facilitates a meeting with the placement and local reentry team to determine the discharge date for the youth
- *Coordination and Communication:* The Therapist connects the placement and the PO or Caseworker through ongoing communication and coordination
- *Community Based Action Team:* The Team is developed to prepare for the youth's return home

SERVICE FOR YOUTH DISCHARGED FROM OUT-OF-HOME CARE

- *Family Therapy:* Additional sessions continue at home or in the community
- *Case Management Services:* Services include: coordination with PO and Caseworker, school reentry, job placement, physical and mental health referrals, links with identified mentor
- *Discharge Summary:* A summary of services is provided
- *Red Flag Checklist:* An individualized Relapse Prevention list for families that is reviewed at 30, 60, and 90 days post discharge from the PLL program. Tune-up sessions are available as indicated

OUTCOMES

PLL is recognized as an evidence-based program by SAMHSA's National Registry of Evidence-Based Programs and Practices (NREPP) and OJJDP's Model Programs Guide. Youth completing PLL services are significantly less likely than youth completing traditional reentry services to be arrested or readjudicated for a felony offense within 12 months of program completion.

Winokur, K. (March 2011). Parenting with Love and Limits (PLL) Re-Entry Services: Evaluation Summary. Tallahassee, FL.: Justice Research Center

www.gopll.com

Dreams Differed

EPILOGUE

DR. CORNELL WHITE TELLS THAT LIFE WITHOUT MEANING, HOPE AND LOVE BREEDS A COLD HEART, MEAN-SPIRITED OUTLOOKS THAT DESTROY BOTH THE INDIVIDUALS AND OTHERS. ALL AROUND THE WORLD, PEOPLE IN SIMILAR CIRCUMSTANCES HAVE REFLECTION THAT ARE SWEET OR SOUR PENDING THEIR POSITION IN LIFE. I SHOULD HAVE, WOULD HAVE, OR COULD HAVE A COMMON CONSIDERATIONS GIVEN TO "DREAMS DIFFERED" (*LANGSTON HUGHES*). THE FOLLOWING BRIEF BIOS GIVE MEANING TO LANGSTON'S WORDS YET UNDERSTAND THAT LIFE CONTINUES AFTER MISTAKES ARE MADE, THAT LOVE LOVE IS ETERNAL. THROUGH FAITH AND EFFORTS, DREAMS BECOME REALITY IN DUE TIME.

JAMES WHITE, AKA: TRAP - WHEN HE WAS LITTLE HE HAD BAD HANDWRITING AND HIS GRANDMOTHER SAID HE SHOULD BE A DOCTOR. HE HAD A GOAL TO MAKE THAT DREAM A REALITY. HE WAS AN HONOR STUDENT AND JUNIOR IN COLLEGE ON HIS WAS TO BECOMING A DOCTOR. HE COULDN'T HANDLE THE STRESS AND DROPPED OUT OF COLLEGE. NOW WITH A SON AND NOWHERE TO TURN HE JOINED MCP WHEN THEY OFFERED HIM THE POSITION OF TREASURER. TODAY HE IS KNOWN AS INMATE #859039.

BRUCE TURNER, AKA: B-DOG - HE SEEMED TO ALWAYS BE INVOLVED IN TROUBLE. FROM DRUG TRAFFICKING TO SHOP LIFTING HE WAS CONTINUOUSLY IN AND OUT OF COURT. THIS HIGH SCHOOL DROPOUT NEVER PLANNED ON LIVING PAST 21 YEARS OF AGE. HE WAS THE COMMUNICATIONS COORDINATOR FOR MCP AND IS NOW KNOWN AS INMATE #759023. HE TURNED 25 TODAY.

JAMAL WILLIAMS, AKA: TINY - THIS SMALL HIGH SCHOOL STUDENT WAS ALWAYS GETTING PICKED ON AND BULLED BY OTHER GANG MEMBERS FOR BEING A LONER AND A NERD. HE TURNED TO MCP WHEN THEY OFFERED HIM PROTECTION IF HE MADE DELIVERIES FOR THEM. HE WAS THE TOP SPOTTER AND CARRIER FOR MCP. HE IS NOW JUST INMATE #596043.

TERRANCE BROWN, AKA: T-MAN - IN HIGH SCHOOL, HE PLAYED MIDDLE LINEBACKER ON THE FOOTBALL TEAM. HE COMPLETED ITT TECHNICAL INSTITUTE AND EARNED AN ASSOCIATE OF APPLIED SCIENCE DEGREE IN THE COMPLETE AUTOMOTIVE TECHNOLOGY PROGRAM. ONCE EMPLOYED, HE WAS TERMINATED AFTER CONTINUOUSLY FAILING THE DRUG SCREENING EMPLOYMENT TEST FOR MARIJUANA. AFTER FAILING REPEATEDLY ON OTHER JOBS, HE GAVE UP AND JOINED MAD CITY POSSE AND BECAME THE GANGS CHIEF ENFORCER. HE IS NOW REFERRED TO AS INMATE #965038.

GRAHAM KING, AKA: G-ROCK - IN HIGH SCHOOL, THIS MERIT ROLL STUDENT WAS THE ANCHOR OF THE TRACK TEAM. HE EARNED A SCHOLARSHIP THAT ONLY LASTED ONE YEAR BECAUSE OF FIGHTING. WITH NO MONEY TO PAY FOR SCHOOL HE GOT INTO DRUG TRAFFICKING. HE WANTED TO BE THE NEXT JOHNNY COCHRAN, BUT BECAME THE LEADER OF THE MCP. HE LIKES **MAKING IT RAIN**, FAST CARS, WOMEN AND HE GOT CAUGHT UP IN THE ROCK STAR LIFESTYLE. FROM LEADER HE BECAME INMATE #684902

OSCAR HOLMES- WAS AN ORIGINAL GANGSTER AND CO-FOUNDER OF THE MAD CITY POSSE. WHEN HE WAS GIVEN A CHOICE TO GO TO COLLEGE OR JAIL BY A JUDGE, HE TURNED TO SCHOOL. NOW A **AMERICORPS VISTA** COLLEGE SENIOR MAJORING IN BUSINESS WITH A MINOR IN EDUCATION. HIS GOAL IS TO BECOME A SCHOOL PRINCIPAL AND TO ESTABLISH A FOUNDATION TO HELP KIDS AVOID THE LIFE OF VIOLENCE AND CRIME. HE IS NOW COMMUNITY SERVICE CHAIRMAN OF **ALPHA PHI ALPHA, INC.**

THE **OLYMPIC** CREEDS REMIND US THAT THE MOST IMPORTANT THING IN LIFE IS NOT THE TRIUMPH BUT THE STRUGGLE, AND THAT THE ESSENTIAL THING IS NOT TO HAVE CONQUERED, BUT TO HAVE FOUGHT WELL.

This Little Light of Mine

YOU CAN'T CHANGE YOUR SHORTCOMINGS UNTIL YOU CAN COUNT ON YOURSELF IN SPITE OF THEM. REMEMBER JUST BECAUSE A PERSON ENGAGES IN A NEGATIVE BEHAVIOR, RELAPSE, OR *"BACKSLIDES"* DOESN'T MEAN THAT THEY DON'T LOVE THEMSELVES. AT TIMES LIFE HAS A WAY OF BEATING DOWN THE VERY BEST OF US; AT THAT POINT WE BEGIN TO QUESTION THE VERY MEANING OF LIFE.

BUT LIKE THE FISHERS OF MEN, A PERSON THAT BELIEVES IN A *"HIGHER POWER"* HAS A REASON TO HOPE. ACKNOWLEDGE AND ACCEPT THE CONSEQUENCES, MOVE PAST THE BLAME AND SHAME GAME. ONCE YOU CHOOSE TO LOVE, YOU CAN LEARN TO FORGIVE YOURSELF.

"1 CORINTHIANS, CHAPTER 15 VERSE 10" – BY DIVINE GRACE TOWARD ME WAS NOT INEFFECTIVE. IN OTHER WORDS, WITHIN EACH OF US IS A SPARK THAT IS THE WAY TO PRODUCTIVE AND HEALTHY LIFE.

Brighter Days Ahead, Scribe L.C.

LISTED BELOW ARE THE PUBLICATIONS OF SOCIAL SKILLS & VIOLENCE PREVENTION WORKBOOKS FROM OUR PARTNER *THE SOCIETY FOR PREVENTION OF VIOLENCE*. PLEASE SEND A CHECK OR PURCHASE ORDER WITH YOUR ORDER AND WE CAN SHIP YOUR ORDER TO YOU, COST: $29.95 PER LESSON

THE READY-TO-USE SOCIAL SKILLS LESSONS & ACTIVITIES
BY: RUTH WELTMANN BEGUN, EDITOR

THIS IS A UNIQUE SERIES CONSISTING OF FOUR VOLUMES. IT GIVES TEACHERS, PARENTS, AND SPECIALISTS A STIMULATING SYSTEMATIC WAY TO DEVELOP POSITIVE SOCIAL BEHAVIORS IN STUDENTS AT ALL LEVELS OF ABILITY AND FOR ALL GRADES. THE FULL SERIES INCLUDES OVER 250 TESTED LESSONS AND SELF-CONTAINED, REPRODUCIBLE WORKSHEETS IN FOUR SEPARATELY PRINTED, SELF-CONTAINED VOLUMES, EACH TAILORED TO THE DEVELOPMENTAL NEEDS OF STUDENTS AT A PARTICULAR GRADE LEVEL: PREK-K, 1-3, 4-6, AND 7-12. THE LESSONS, ACTIVITIES, AND PRACTICE WORKSHEETS ARE BASED ON REAL-LIFE SITUATIONS AND HELP BUILD CHILDREN'S SELF-ESTEEM, SELF-CONTROL, RESPECT FOR THE RIGHTS OF OTHERS, AND A SENSE OF RESPONSIBILITY FOR ONE'S OWN ACTIONS.

PREK-K

GRADES 1-3

GRADES 4-6

GRADES 7-12

ELEMENTARY

SECONDARY

EACH VOLUME INCLUDES AN INTRODUCTION TO THE CURRICULUM AND LESSON FORMAT. . . .BRIEF GUIDELINES "TO THE TEACHER" FOR USING THE ACTIVITIES MOST EFFECTIVELY. . . .REPRODUCIBLE TASK REVIEW CARDS FOR CIRCLE-TIME CLASS DISCUSSIONS. . . .AND A FAMILY TRAINING BOOKLET ADDRESSED TO PARENTS WITH SUGGESTIONS FOR TEACHING SOCIAL SKILLS AT HOME (IN BOOKS PREK TO 6).

MISSION

THE SOCIETY FOR PREVENTION OF VIOLENCE IS DEDICATED TO REDUCING THE PREVALENCE OF VIOLENT ACTS AND ASOCIAL BEHAVIOR OF CHILDREN AND ADULTS THROUGH EDUCATION. IT ACCOMPLISHES THIS MISSION BY TEACHING CHILDREN AND ADULTS THE USE OF SKILLS NECESSARY TO BUILD THEIR CHARACTER AND HELP THEM ACQUIRE A STRONG VALUE SYSTEM. SPV MOTIVATES LEARNERS TO DEVELOP THEIR COMMUNICATION SKILLS AND TO REALIZE GROWTH IN INTERPERSONAL RELATIONSHIPS. THE MISSION INCLUDES INTEGRATION OF SOCIAL AND ACADEMIC SKILLS TO ENCOURAGE THOSE WHO USE THEM TO REACH THEIR FULL POTENTIAL AND CONTRIBUTE TO OUR NATION'S SOCIETY BY BEING ABLE TO MAKE DECISIONS AND SOLVE PROBLEMS THROUGH EFFECTIVE AND APPROPRIATE MEANS.

FOR MORE INFORMATION VISIT OUR SITE AT: *WWW.SPVOHIO.ORG*, CALL US AT: *216.591.1876*, FAX US AT: *216.591.1879*, FAX US AT: *4645 RICHMOND RD - CLEVELAND, OH 44128*

THE FIRE CROTCH PLAGUE

LET IT RIDE • GAME READY 4 LIFE PRESENTS:

THE CONDOM BOWL AN * EM

Makin' It Rain Condom Style

FEATURING ART BY:
DANIELLE LADOVICH

SCRIBE DERRICK J. TURNER

WH✷A!
DO NO HARM

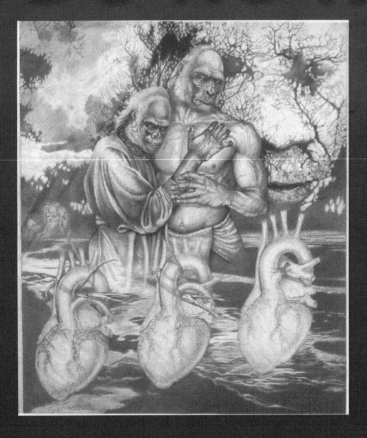

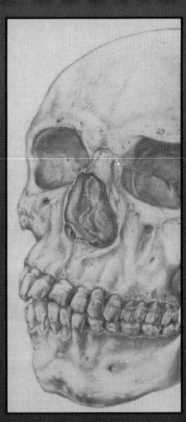

THE TIMELESS TALES OF HEALERS, ALCHEMISTS, SORCERERS, SHAMANS, AND PHYSICIANS TO SHOW CONSIDERATION, COMPASSION AND BENEVOLENCE FOR THEIR PATIENTS. WHY CAN'T THEY ALL JUST GET ALONG?

WRITTEN BY SCRIBE L.C. AND ILLUSTRATED BY MARK MCQUEEN JR. AND LEONARD CHARLES LEE COLLINS.

Seek **H**im **F**irst **M**inistries

Stop The Violence
A Father's Perspective

One wrong choice, one wrong decision,
one wrong moment,
one act of violence stole my Son from me forever,
on March 5, 2013 I lost my son to one act of Violence
shot to death at the age of 23 on the Streets of Cleveland, Ohio.

One wrong choice, one wrong decision, one wrong moment,
one act of violence stole the legacy of my name,
One wrong choice, one wrong decision, One wrong moment,
one act of violence stole the precious moments
that a father has to spend with a son,

one wrong choice, one wrong decision, one wrong moment,
one act of violence stole the seed of my seed.
One wrong choice, one wrong decision,
one wrong moment, one wrong act.
Stop the Violence

The wrong choice, equals a wrong act,
the wrong decision affects you and everyone around you
the wrong moment, affects our future.
Make this your Defining Moment to embrace the greatness within you
To stop the Violence

Now to Him who is able to do exceedingly abundantly above all that we ask or think,
according to the power that works in us. Ephesians 3:20
Elder Marcus Lawrence

Seek Him First Ministries
Pastor Marion & Elder Marcus Lawrence
Embracing Greatness
When in Cleveland the Cleveland Area
Come out and Worship with us at
4342 E. 71st
Cleveland, Ohio
(between Harvard and Grant)
(234)678-0609
Sunday Morning Worship Service 11:00 a.m.
Thursday Discipline Kingdom Saints Bible Study 6:00 p.m.
www.seekhimfirstministries.org

To the Fathers out there dealing with a similar loss
HOLLA AT ME FOR SUPPORT EACH OTHER AT
Elderlawrence816@gmail.com
But seek ye first the Kingdom of God and all of his righteousness. Matthew 6:33

Complicity
Eye Of The Storm

Scribe L.C. takes you on a journey that makes you ask yourself how can I help my community. "Complicity Eye of The Storm" is a tragic tale of Original Gangster Oscar Holmes, who is forced with the prospect of avenging his brothers' murder or earning his degree. "Complicity" is based on the real-life experiences of inmates of Mansfield Correctional Institution.

"This story should be on the "must read" list for every youth person. Our children make up 30 percent of our population, yet are one hundred percent of our future. Every step that they make offers a choice. Do they travel the "right" path or the "wrong" path? Do they choose school or person? Do they look for God or a gang leader? Do they pick up books or guns? The choice that they hopefully make will be education over violence. A good job over prison sentence. A loving family over a bunch of other inmates. A life of happiness over a "life sentence". Choice may not always be easy, but the "right choice" will be worth it!"

Kenny Yuko
Former State Representative

Other works of the Scribe Nation

Medusa Chronicles: Revenge In Blue

Stolen Moments: The Yvonne Pointer Story

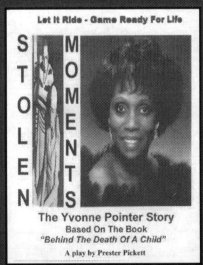

Cover art provided by: Mark McQueen Jr. and Leonard Charles Lee Collins

Just Chillin' Books
Cleveland Treatment Center, 1127 Carnegie Ave, Cleveand, OH 44115